SHOPKEEPING

SHOPKEEPING

STORIES, ADVICE, AND OBSERVATIONS

PETER MILLER, bookseller

PA PRESS

PRINCETON ARCHITECTURAL PRESS · NEW YORK

Published by
Princeton Architectural Press
A division of Chronicle Books LLC
70 West 36th Street, New York, NY 10018
papress.com

Editor: Jennifer N. Thompson
Designer: Paul Wagner

Library of Congress Cataloging-in-Publication Data
Names: Miller, Peter, 1946– author.
Title: Shopkeeping : stories, advice, and observations / Peter Miller.
Description: First edition. | New York : Princeton Architectural Press,
    [2024] | Includes bibliographical references. | Summary:
    "A love letter to the shop by beloved bookseller Peter Miller"
    —Provided by publisher.
Identifiers: LCCN 2023027522 | ISBN 9781797228761 (hardcover)
    | ISBN 9781797228778 (ebook)
Subjects: LCSH: Retail trade—Anecdotes. | Specialty stores—Anecdotes.
    | Miller, Peter, 1946—Anecdotes.
Classification: LCC HF5429 .M498 2024 | DDC 658.8/7—dc23/
    eng/20230912
LC record available at https://lccn.loc.gov/2023027522

CONTENTS

10   AN ARCHITECT'S FOREWORD
        Steven Holl

13   INTRODUCTION
        Some Sense, and Some Sense of

19   Chapter 1
        TO BE A RETAILER

22   Chapter 2
        TO OPEN

26   Chapter 3
        WHAT IS A SHOP?
        Obstructions · When You Are Trying to
        Find a Shop

40   Chapter 4
        THE DETAILS OF SPACE
        Packaging · Specifics · A Show of Names ·
        Display · Gardening · What Have You ·
        Certain Days

60   Chapter 5
        SEEING TIME
        People Come · Passing the Time · Once Upon ·
        A Terrible Location · Street Tales

74   Chapter 6
        THE NATURE OF SPACE—DOG ON A PORCH
        Cups and Surfaces · The Ten Best · Light ·
        How Do You Look

86   Chapter 7
        COUNTERS
        Two Salts · Time on Paper · Where Leads
        Will Lead · Miracles and Spirits

100   Chapter 8
        TO MOVE
        Language of a Shop

104   Chapter 9
        THE ELECTRONICS OF IT
        Posts, Email, or Other · Electronic Issues
        and Repair · Inventory · In a Sense ·
        The Big Shops · A Very New Kind of Retail ·
        To Carry Radios · Locking the Door

126   Chapter 10
COMMERCE
When You See a Shop · What Are You ·
Shops Today · New Shops ·
Times Square · Shopkeeping Aside /
Last Notes · The New Days ·
On the Thought of Opening a Shop

139   ACKNOWLEDGMENTS

141   A BOOK LIST

"

We have to know
that we want lively,
well-used streets
and other public
spaces, and why we
want them.

—Jane Jacobs

"

AN ARCHITECT'S FOREWORD

I met Peter Miller in 1979 when he first opened Peter Miller Books in Seattle. I had just moved to New York City, returning to the Pacific Northwest several times a year to visit my parents in Manchester, Washington.

Passing through Seattle to visit Peter and his shop was a joy I never missed. His space has always been much more than an architectural bookstore—it's a cultural space of education, meeting, and interaction. It's a space radiating the joys of life via Peter's contagious enthusiasm. Often when I would stop in, Peter would cook up a superb pasta lunch on a hot plate in the back room. He would pour us each wine in special glasses from Scandinavia he sold in the shop. (When the pandemic hit, I ordered twelve of these glasses delivered to New York.)

Students of architecture can learn a lot from Peter; he reminds me of my teacher Astra Zarina. When I was her student in Rome in 1970, she told me: "If you want to be an architect, first you must learn how to cook!"

In his attention to detail, Peter thinks like the best architects. The details are important in direct relation to how people experience them in actual space. There is a story about one of Alvar Aalto's last project, a grand piano practice room. For its geometry, Aalto asked the pianist, "When you finish practicing, which way do you walk around the piano?"

Peter Miller Books has always been in Seattle, and now it is on a unique urban site: Seattle's Alaskan Way Viaduct, a double-deck concrete freeway section only 2.2 miles long, opened in 1953, cutting the city off from Elliott Bay. This blockage of the urban waterfront was finally completely removed in 2019, being replaced by a tunnel. Peter Miller moved his bookstore to an urban alley below the viaduct in 2015, and now it is part of the urban transformation of Pioneer Square.

Steven Holl
Rhinebeck, NY
December 12, 2022

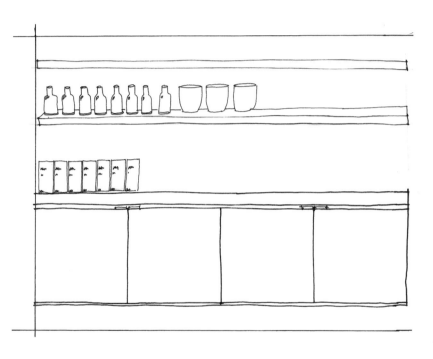

INTRODUCTION:
SOME SENSE, AND SOME SENSE OF

You never get to hear from a shopkeeper. Here are some thoughts, and notions, and what I have learned in forty-five years of shopkeeping.

A shopkeeper straddles the bow of the ship. They are the first to sense a tide. Each day, they have a shop to open.

At the deck of running a shop, you need to know what can help, what to look out for, what to hope for, and what you can do.

This is a manual, of sorts, of shopkeeping tasks.

There is a tradition of shopkeeping, a tradition of codes, etiquette, and customs. For the most part, it is an oral history, passed along person to person. You learn to be a retailer not by going to college, but by going to work. You learn from people who have learned how to run a shop.

I have stood in a shop in Paris, in a shop in Venice, in a shop in Helsinki and watched as each shopkeeper managed the affairs of running a shop. And realized, in the best shops, they were conducting an honors course of shopkeeping.

Watch for a moment—how each person coming into the shop is greeted, how questions are handled, how attentions are directed. Watch how the counter is cleaned or the credit card handled. Watch how each customer is respected.

I asked a shopkeeper in Venice, the busiest of cities, if she said hello to each person who came in the shop. She said, "Of course, how could we not?"—and goodbye, do you also say goodbye to each? She laughed and said, "Well of course, how could we not, and we say thank you, as well. They are our customers, our living."

The best pen shop in Milan is near the Galleria. It is a master class for the design of a pen shop. Where one must stand, how the pens must look, how the counter must be clear and clean, where the less expensive pens must reside. A thousand details, made and improved a thousand times so that the shop will be ready to open, to greet its customers.

There must be small pads to try out a pen, and they must always be unmarked, and they must not create a mess. If it is a high-end pen shop, then the lighting must not be general, it must be specific.

As you stand there, it is as if each counter were set, made like a careful bed is made. You can walk the length of each counter—there are four of them—and look at the different series of pens and pencils. No one

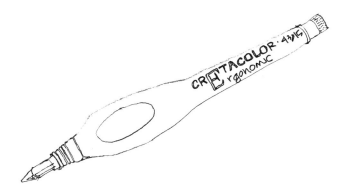

will say a word. But if you look up, someone will quietly ask, "Yes, may I help you?"

You are shopping for pens; it is a great honor, and one that they share with you. If they are very good, then they will learn, with a few short questions, what it is that you know and what it is that you need.

There are no books on shopkeeping. A few design manuals, a few recollections and looking-backs, but little more. Much of the world, of course, works in retail, of one sort or another.

We walk to look at the shops, we dress up to visit them, we feel our own excitement when we go into them.

Shops are the measure of a town. In your mind, you keep careful track of your best and favorite shops. You judge a city by them. When you are in the city and when you think of the city, it is the shops that best organize your plans. You judge your civilization by them.

You expect them to be there; you expect them to be good at what they do.

A good shop is more literal than sentimental.

& Diaries, Desks &
Chairs, Desktop Instruments
& Accessories, Fine
Papers, Greeting & Note Cards,

Lighting, Notebooks &
Journals, Pouches &
Cases, Prints & Posters, Stock &
Custom Stationery,
AND Writing Implements

MCNALLY JACKSON STORE

GOODS for the STUDY

—1—

TO BE A RETAILER

never tell anyone to be a retailer. It is a fragile occupation and hard on your heart. You put on the same show, each day, and hope that you have chosen well, that it is what people might want. You worry and you wonder and, for much of the time, you are alone with your decisions.

When I was in graduate school in Boston, we went to a bar that showed cowboy westerns on Thursday evenings. The owner came out through a set of mock curtains and told us what the movie would be. I laughed and thought, that is what a retailer is, hoping the show is good and that people will come.

You are the strongest and weakest part of the business. You have only to look at a retail space that has closed. You are the breath; your spirit has created what would otherwise not be there. It is your optimism, your belief, that created the shop and that keeps it alive. Should you lose that, then the business is done.

Should you lose heart, your staff will know it. They cannot be that heart. They can support and sustain it, but they cannot be it. And your customers will know, and they will slowly lose their attachment.

I remember a customer taking me aside and asking if everything was okay. I said yes, because it was mostly okay, but his doubt had been touched by some books having been left out of place, books that had simply not made it to their location.

It made him nervous for the shop. We were typically very careful to keep a specific order—he had noticed a lapse in that order and it distracted him.

The best interior designer in Seattle's history, Jean Jongeward, would often come to the shop in its quietest moments. She would arrive, open her wonderful big smile, point out that no one was there, and say "Well, I guess that it all falls on me." And then she would stack books up on the counter, to be delivered to her office.

— 2 —

TO OPEN

When I come to the shop in the morning, I always walk in with some slight caution. I check the door and the windows, I check the shop front where it meets the sidewalk, I smell the space, as I walk in.

A shop is at anchor, in a sense—weather and people and nature, all are in its province. It sits alone. It can be touched and peered through, it can be broken, pushed, marked, disfigured, admired, photographed. You can leave messages on its door, or bang to get its attention. It is not like an office—it is in the passage of people and the passage of time. You can ask to be let in, you can simply go in, you can nearly insist to be let in.

It has heat and moisture; it has leaks and cracks; it has high and low ground; it has faced the night, every night; it has met the wind, taken the driving rain, cracked and dried; it has sat.

Last summer, the highway department drilled deeply into the waterfront for the new transportation tunnel. The rats were driven uphill, toward the buildings. For several weeks, there was a single, uncertain rat running about the floor of the shop. In the morning, slipped under the door, there were handwritten notes of concern: *We saw a rat in your shop.*

Before we even called for help, the city sent an animal control team. They explained what had caused the sudden flurry of rat sightings. And promised that they would be able to help.

Somehow, the authorities convinced the rat to give up the public stage. The siege was ended; the rat returned to a more private world.

A shop is a stage—there is a degree to which it must be ready. If it is not ready, if there is a stray box on the floor, a customer will flinch and fear they are not to come in. If a light bulb is out, they will fear something is wrong. A clear-countered kitchen, a couch with fresh pillows, a well-made bed—that is a shop, ready to open.

The shop does not need to be perfect—but it must at least appear to be ready, a small, specific distinction. Years ago, there was a leak from the space above us— and our shop filled with three inches of warm water from the hot water tank. The books bent and warped, the carpet sponged, the windows were fogged. We had ten humidifiers and blowers and power cords, set in all directions, to begin the cleanup. And insurance agents, several of them, making notes.

But still people came and they stood at the book- cases looking at books, even bent books. The store looked somehow ready, even though their feet were wet and the walls were damp.

It reminded me of the famous black-and-white photo of a London bookshop after an aerial assault in World War II. The roof was gone, you could see the sky, but people were still standing in front of the bookcases, looking at the titles and reading.

— 3 —

WHAT IS A SHOP?

A shop is a space that happens to be public. It is not a bench to sit on in the park. It is not a shelter, like a bus stop. You cannot bring your horse into a shop.

In formal terms, it is an exhibit. You do not need a ticket, but there are details of decorum—one must be respectful, not loud; any liquids must be capped; no intrusive electronics. It is not someone's home, but it is someone's shop.

You do not need to order something, nor even to explain why you have come in. You do not need a reservation. You do not even need a purpose. You come to a shop because it has something you need, or simply to see what it has.

What do you sell here? they often ask, or *Is there any particular order to the store?*

A town or city is a private affair. You can walk its length and tour its parks. You can admire and judge its surfaces. But the majority of a town or city, its offices and residence and services, is private. You do not casually walk into them. A restaurant or even a coffee shop is an invitation, but you cannot go in without buying something. A hair salon is useless (being both private and intimate), though more useful than an event space, which is profoundly useless. And you certainly cannot go into the police station.

A shop will make some people nervous. They do not know how to act or behave or, in some cases, feel. Curiously, everyone seems to know that they are allowed into a shop. However, they do not know if they are allowed to touch anything.

A true shop has bearing, and some attitude, gentle as it may be. A true shop may or may not be kind to children; it may or may not love dogs. That depends on the shop and the history. They may have had some very difficult children, some very difficult dogs.

When I opened Peter Miller Books forty-five years ago, people came and said it was a nice shop but they only bought their books from Rizzoli, in New York. (Years later, when Rizzoli offered me a leadership position in their shop, I felt I had closed some distance.)

When you enter a shop, when you come aboard, so to speak, it is a help if you say hello, and when you leave, it is a courtesy to say goodbye. And perhaps thank you.

No one will tell you that. But I must admit, when people come and walk all the way through the shop and then walk out without a word, I am always, at the least, surprised.

Obstructions

When I was in graduate school, I took a job at the Mount Auburn Hospital in Cambridge, Massachusetts, as a night shift orderly in the emergency room. It was the late 1960s, a time of some chaos and rebellion. In terms of the hospital, nothing seemed affected, in any particular way, but we were very busy—Cambridge, at that time, was a very busy place.

One hot and humid late Friday evening, as I was cleaning up the sheets and medical debris from a small cleanse-and-stitch operation, I heard a very distinct and loud voice in the hall ask, "Who is in charge here?" in a way that was more demand than inquiry. I was the very lowest on the totem pole of emergency room staff, so I could come and go practically unnoticed. I walked out to the hall and looked to see who was taking up so much room. It was a very handsome and impatient doctor—a quite famous heart surgeon. It was his turn to do emergency room duty, on a summer's Friday night no less, when, as he told us all, he should be out sailing.

To make matters and coincidence much worse, the very next patient, wheeled abruptly in on a gurney from the back end of an ambulance, was an eighty-two-year-old man with an acute heart problem. The man's wife was desperately holding his hand; he was holding on to his Red Sox baseball cap and softly moaning with pain. The famous surgeon could not believe it. It was as if the problem had been waiting specifically for him.

In moments, a medical team was assembled, an operating room was booked, and two of the three nurses were conscripted into heart operation duty. "Is this all we have?" the surgeon grumbled, and then he turned on me. "You come, too!" It reminded me of last-second emergency hikes that were sometimes needed—I had for three summers worked near the Presidential Range in New Hampshire and there had been a couple of "grab your gear, someone is lost in the mountains" emergencies.

I went up to the intensive care floor with the nurses. They showed me how to wash up and scrub and slip into the operating room gear. In only moments, we were in the operating room itself, and moments later, they had begun. I stood to the back. In short order, they had the chest opened and the leaks under control, and I heard the surgeon say, "Ah, there it is!"

"Come here, kid," he said to me, and I came over, not without some nervousness, and peered into the open chest, and he was right: there it was. Right in the middle of lines and veins and muscles and pink fat was this unsightly blob, the aneurysm, this unsightly bulge of clotted blood along the aorta. It looked so out of place and out of color and unhealthy that any school kid would have known it was the trouble.

It was a tricky, skillful business, cutting out the bulge and repairing the blood supply, but once it was done, it certainly looked much healthier. They closed the patient back up, the surgeon rushed out to catch the first light of Saturday sailing, and I helped clean up the mess of such an operation.

I know they did not have great hopes for the operation. But four days later, my beeper went off and I went up to the ICU and there was the aneurysm patient, with a big smile and sitting up, with his Red Sox cap on and his wife holding his hand. He had heard I was a part of the operation and wanted to say thank you. I laughed and said I was hardly a part, I was just a fan.

The image of that aneurysm, literally a blockage in otherwise working parts, never left me. I think of it at the weirdest, often mechanical, times—when the vacuum stops working, when the store seems stalled and dull, when there seems no way that the finances will ever keep pace with the costs, when the computers mutiny. And it seems to help, this image that there is a buildup of stuff, of dirt and clot and error and age, and if I can just get to it, if I can carefully clean it and get things uncovered and able to run fairly, then it will repair itself—or at least have a chance to.

It is the great difficulty of running a shop—the fragility of your own confidence and optimism. You are the steward of an invented form, and it is your huff and puff that gives it life. You are but a fraction away, a blockage or a break or even a quiet slowness from chewing on your own arm. You have chosen the absurdly risky occupation of relying upon people coming through the door for your lifeblood. (Odd as it might seem, there is a certain parallel to playing golf—golf, a truly invented form, is the enactment of immediate risk. Each time you hit the ball, you are but a fraction away from threatening your own confidence. In a sense, golf is a mini drama, a kind of practicing the scales of risk.)

It is not uncommon to hear ex-shopkeepers, scarred by the memory, declaring they will never set such a brick-and-mortar stage again. Curiously, the internet has lured perfectly sensible private citizens into a notion that they should become retailers. It is, apparently, a siren call to people who, for the most part, had never heard even a retail note before. They can sell things without having to meet or say good day to any humans! They do not have to know any of them.

Who would have guessed investment bankers would be selling shoes, or electric drills, or jewelry, or pots and pans, or underwear? Who would have guessed that so many people who knew nothing about retail, nothing at all, and never cared to, who in fact and in history do not like retail, do not themselves even like going to a shop, who do not like the idiom of customers, who do not like even saying good morning when they do walk into a shop—who would have guessed that these very people would start companies to sell things?

If you travel, there are many places in the world that still preserve a sense of having shops. Italy and France, of course; Belgium and Holland, some of Germany, all of Scandinavia. New Zealand and Australia—how dearly they have labored to keep shops and the sense of shops and the responsibility of shops alive; there are rows of dress shops in Sydney and stationery stores in every town in New Zealand. Tokyo loves its shops; Mexico City and Barcelona and Buenos Aires all know it is their exceptional shops that fuel their vitality.

Common to all is a faint and remarkable detail: they all will greet their customer, however modestly. They all will nod or smile or slightly bow, they all will acknowledge the morning or the day or your presence. And, for the most part, they will all acknowledge your departure. It is not an easy detail to maintain. For one thing, it is, as are most of the details of courtesy and manners, quite slow: it simply takes time. The French are brilliant with their hellos; they know perfectly that wagering even a fraction of extra emotion or sound is not sustainable. There are too many customers and too many who will not be buying, who do not know enough to buy, or who think they know

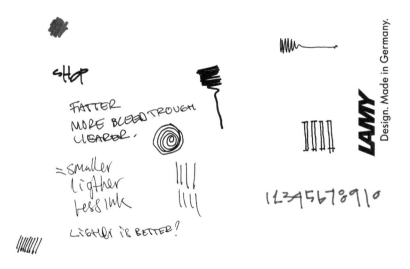

SHOP

FATTER
MORE BLEED TROUGH
CLEARER.

= smaller
lighter
less ink

LIGHTER IS BETTER?

1234567890

too much to buy. The French even keep score. If you do not answer their hello, they will make a mark against you in their minds. You may not notice, but the mark is there, until you, too, say hello.

There is also the very true threat of the new customer, who has little or no tradition for going into shops and, in some cases, little use for learning such a tradition. They will walk right through a "Good morning," they will be suspicious of a "Please let me know if I can help," and they will leave with not a sign or signal, as if they had not indeed come in but were simply ever on the sidewalk. And you must be careful: you can feel the fool for saying hello, and no one wants to be the fool. It is a kind of invasion of the nothing-matters. And, if nothing matters, then, of course, your shop does not matter. You learn to be careful, to protect your shop but also to protect your tradition and your heart. For that is what keeps you open.

When You Are Trying to Find a Shop

I love Stockholm. My daughter and her family live there. For each of my visits, she has a collection of new shops to show me—a gallery of paper, a pen shop, a small wine shop, a design shop, a soap and cosmetics shop, a new cheese shop. I can send you to a bakery that is so good it is worth an entire trip.

On one visit, we wanted to find a particular line of sweatpants, Resteröds, to bring back as Christmas gifts. Every supplier that we called was out of stock. We had one last place to try.

It was on the corner of a quiet, residential street. They had shop windows on both sides, showing hundreds of socks and sets of underwear and T-shirts and even girdles and scarves. It was a colorful, motley crew and reminded me of the era of Lucille Ball and Xavier Cugat and Carmen Miranda circa 1954. Inside, there was only room for about eight people. There were already eight people inside, pressed up looking at the display cases of underwear and pajamas and every brand of sock and T-shirt.

Behind the counter, behind the three people trying to help all of us, were boxes and boxes and boxes, stacked high up to the fourteen-foot-high pressed-tin ceiling. Some of the boxes were askew, some were open, and some had advertisements next to them, a last chance to lure you to their particular T-shirt.

I nearly forgot, there were also bathrobes and work shirts and sweaters. There was no room for anything to get more than a folded display, so it looked like a crowd trying its best, in folded form, to get just a bit ahead of the others, to elbow to the front.

It was late now, nearly closing time on a November Saturday. It might as well have been the sale of the year. It took ten minutes to get some help and by then more people had come in behind us.

They did have Resteröds, so we bought sweatpants (no one asked a size, they simply looked at you) and four pairs of cotton gloves and knitted caps and tights, I think. It was all a big package and off we went, leaving a full shop behind, as if no one had left.

Now, here I am, wearing those sweatpants, as I type a tale on a winter's Sunday morning. I must say, these are better sweatpants than any I have ever owned. The pockets are true pockets, the cuffs are sewn, and the front ties are thick. It is a thrill to find them in the morning.

I like shopping, but I love shops.

"

There are some
enterprises in
which a careful
disorderliness is the
true method.

—Herman Melville

"

— 4 —

THE DETAILS
OF SPACE

Any shop must be analyzed from its bones to its windows, its floors, and its relation to pedestrians and neighbors and the street. Every detail signals how it wants and hopes to be perceived. You will do the analysis as you are creating the shop—but in a sense, it is a process that you will always be doing. You will always be checking and upgrading the bones.

Forty years ago, we hired Tim Girvin to design our logo. I have always liked it, but more importantly, it has carried its own, on its own.

It has very loyal fans. I remember the buoyant owner of a famous design company, after buying a great stack of books, came back to the shop ten minutes later. He said, I have to tell you, I love your logo. I am going to use something like it for our company—you will probably never see it, but I wanted you to know.

He did love the logo—his version was very similar. For years, people asked me if we had opened a design company.

Packaging

We sell a lot of pens, pencils, erasers, and leads. More now than ever. Soon, I believe, we will sell even more of them, as the world moves into its renaissance. It is always a good sign when the difference is in the details.

I never liked putting pens or pencils, erasers or lead or sharpeners, into paper bags, and always thought they would get lost.

I found a long, clear nine-inch-by-four-inch Ziploc bag and put our square red sticker on the front, and now that is where all the pens and pencils and such go when being sold. It makes each piece particular, and safe, and kept. I know they work—people, and my family, ask for extras for their other pens. I wish I had thought of it thirty years ago.

Specifics

I am fortunate—some of the best architects and designers have helped to detail and design the shop. It has made all the difference. They have often said no when I would have said yes.

When I look at a person's library, I immediately see and know many things. It is the details that I work with every day, the relation of books, of their size and worth and physical needs. It is said that the best garbageman knows everyone on his route intimately. He handles a proportion of their things.

When a good architect looks at a space, at my shop, they see and know hundreds and thousands of things. And that is what can make all the difference.

The height of a door, the frame of a window, the axis of the building, the scale of the floor, the rhythm of the wall, the pattern of entry, the prospect of height, the weight of steel, the touch of wood. There are relations and patterns and parts that create a space. A good designer will see them and feel them and use them: scale, proportion, and form.

We have never had more than a modest budget for shop design. But we have an immodest amount of notions. I can show you crucial details that came out of what was done.

We are currently trying to design a space, just outside in the hall, that would allow the stationery and pens a better stage, a more distinct presentation. In the 1930 Stockholm Exposition, the architect Sigurd Lewerentz designed a series of retail stands, a kind of hybrid of a newsstand and a pop-up shop. They each had large, playful graphics, broad sides of color, and inventive perspectives.

Whatever we settle on, it must have a careful sense and effect. Stationery—in all its details—has a very different weight and permanence. It is approached differently than books. And each piece that will be on display is precisely distinct.

There have been many drawings and many variations, even though the addition is only five feet wide and twelve feet long. Only architecture can do this. Only an architect will find it fascinating to hunt and labor for precisely the proper answer.

It is possible to argue for weeks about shelf height. But the design of a shop is more complex than preferences. It is literally architecture, in the longest, quietest sense.

When the computer industry was beginning to open retail shops, there were two basic approaches. Microsoft hired a consulting firm to lay out their shop space. No one remembers a Microsoft shop.

Apple hired an architecture firm to design its space. The Apple stores are now quite famous.

At its base, every shop is a flower shop or a fruit stand. The differences are in the details of the stand and the details of the products.

A Show of Names

From the back room to signage, from shipping to storage, a good shop is an act of intention and design. As you enter and pass within a shop, your own radar signals the hot and the cold, the yes and the no, the specific and the blurred. Typically, when you come to the back of a shop, you become less interested.

As an experiment, walk into any retail space, and walk every aisle and every corner. Then, if I give you

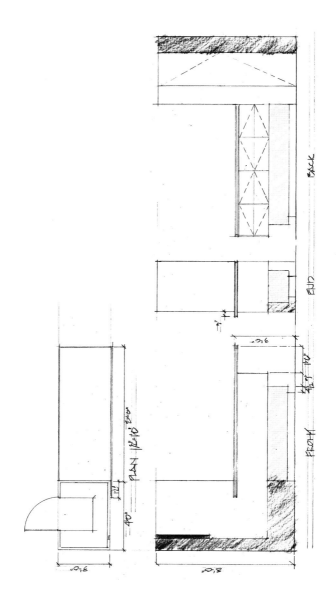

BACK

END

FRONT

PLAN 1'4"×10'×10"

46

a floor plan, and colored pencils, and ask that you describe each area—red or yellow for yes, green or blue for maybe, brown or black for no—you will find that you do think something of each space and each passage. You feel a yes or you feel a no or you simply pass through.

Kathy Wesselman designed the signage for our shop. It desperately needed her, stuck back in an alley with no other retail and not even an obvious front. Somehow, with a touch here, a piece there, a high piece in the middle and a red interior door, she made it seem sensible. Signage is like music—you must be good at it for it to be good. Then it is a treat.

A shop is a restaurant with no seats nor menus that serves neither food nor drink. It is a bakery with no baked goods.

It is a lemonade stand that sells the proper glasses, and the lemons and the sugar and the ice perhaps and even the spoons, the knives, and the cutting board. But not the lemonade.

Display

It is my version of flower arrangement to lay out the books. It is such an obscure version of design that I rarely talk about it. Who would sit for such a lecture?

But here are a few of the details. Books are shy. They take longer than everyone else. They spend most of their lives vertically on a shelf, spine side out, with only a title and author and a publisher's icon to announce them. They open, and open up, only if you open them. They cannot take any sun or liquid at all. Even a copy of *King Lear* can be outshouted by a rubber duck. Books are shy.

When they do get time on the center table, it should be quality time. Books, like flowers, come in many shapes and sizes and colors, and getting all of that to appear at its best can be a difficulty.

You can make piles of each title. You can put like-minded authors or subjects together in a series. But you must also have the less expensive books to the front, you must keep the heavier books away from the edge, you must leave enough room that each is unique, and you must quietly match the direction of the spines.

Look for patterns: cycles of color, or typeface, or graphics; thickness or surface. Make terms with the variants; they represent each in particular as well as the whole. There are rules—there are not, of course, rules—but there are rules. There is no class that you can take, but there are rules.

For example, in floral arrangement, you would not put three tulips together with forsythia without considering their relations. Yes, you can do it, you can even

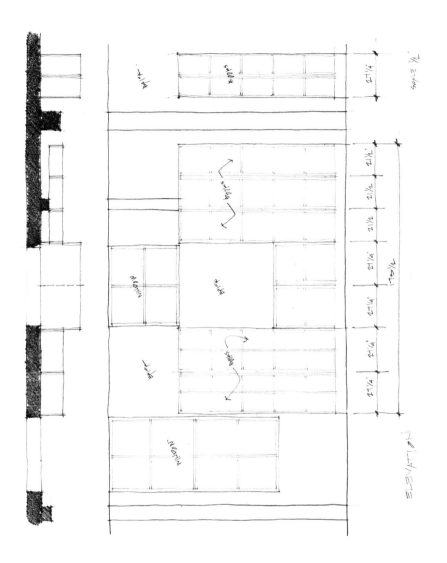

ELEVATION

49

bravely do it, but it takes fiddling. The forsythia can be a chorus and the tulips, if they are the proper color, can be the speakers.

Ring a tall wide vase with the lovely forsythia and allow the tulips to emerge. But that is flower arranging. Books are their own kingdom. It might seem that their order is unimportant, irrelevant, or even vain, but that is not the truth. They are simply shy.

As you see them on the table, there are patterns. As a fork looks foolish pointing toward the diner, so too must the books be in a form that one can approve. Move the two small white ones, I might say, next to each other—they are both arguing a similar case. Or leave the three very bulky volumes in series, for the customer will sense that each is a thicker commitment.

You have four titles, all in forms of green landscape, and that will signal a topic, but we are not a clothes shop, so you must add other landscaping books or it will seem dull. The large photo book cannot stay on the table—it has wonderful nudes among its photos. You will have customers laying coats across the other books or staying too long. It must have a little privacy but not, of course, too much. And so forth.

Book arranging, or any retail display, is a little like manners—it is simple and complicated. At its worst, it

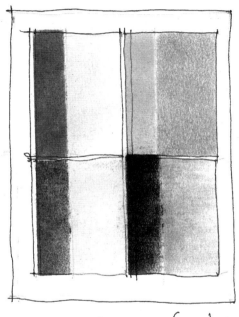

interaction of color

is retail manipulation, best calculated in any airport kiosk. They have only a moment to make their pitch.

At its best, display is order and form, presenting a fair review of its case, the task of any good presentation. For reference and inspiration, sometimes I sit with Albers's *Interaction of Color*, to have even a sip of the best minds.

The fiction it takes to run a shop is a fragile boundary. Should you lose any of the fiction, a shop can suddenly seem to not be a very good idea at all.

Gardening

A good shopkeeper will notice if a wall or section is in a slump or distress, as any gardener would. You will scan the displays and the cases with the wand of your mind, checking, in a way, for life and breath.

A gardener would look for ground that has become too hard, or soil that needs enriching or shading or watering. So too, a shop owner must sense if the book or product is in the wrong place, or with the wrong things, or being shown incorrectly to make its presence best felt.

It is more a clear sense than a science. We keep the pens and pencils and paper, and their displays, well away from the books. When someone is considering a Caran d'Ache leadholder or the proper sharpener for their wooden pencils, or the correct eraser, they are using a particular part of their brain. And it is a slightly different part than they will use to select a design book.

We have a theory section. It is to the side of the main section—theory takes at least one more beat to be considered. It is not an impulse as much as it is an interest and an inspection.

Similarly, it is foolish to put a $95 art book next to a large selection of $24 books to read right now. It is not unlike wine—when I am hunting for a $24 bottle, I am not in the mood for a $95 version. It is a different attention.

You sense a shop, and it is a pleasure when each section, each turn, seems particular and cared for. And proper.

What Have You

Every piece in a shop is selected. Some, like guidebooks or colored pencils, may have been ordered in series. But for the most part, the selection in a shop is literally specific, piece by piece.

The hard part is keeping a clear sense of what it is you are trying to do. With books, for example, are you trying to feature only current titles, books that are being talked about or promoted?

We carry, on the front table, the slim volume *In Praise of Shadows*, by Jun'ichirō Tanizaki. It was first published in Japan in 1933, as a holiday addendum to his very popular novels. Now, nearly one hundred years later, it is his most famous piece. It is published by a small press, Leete's Island Books, just near New Haven, Connecticut.

We have always carried it and always shall—it is a fascinating study of light and shadow and culture. In a way, it is what we do. But many people have never heard of the book; the publisher is far too modest to do promotion, and many shops have never heard of the book or the publisher.

In a sense, I look at every book that we carry and hope that the book will have the honor and strength that *In Praise of Shadows* has. Some titles simply become a kind of hero. And, to my mind, that gets them some bragging rights.

Jane Jacobs's book *The Death and Life of Great American Cities* was published in 1961. It was a great hit, arguing well and with humor that the cities must show more muscle and steel as they work to make and keep their body and soul strong and healthy. Jacobs is part of a proud tradition of Greenwich Village authors, all characterized by their spirited defense of intelligence, intuition, and diversity. Remarkably, the book is still a hit, and still works, and, as they say, can still dance.

We carry a paperback edition, $18. And a new cloth-bound anniversary edition, from Penguin, for $24. When we can, we have a first edition of the book, for $95, in cloth—it is lovely in its original format. And a $75 cloth-bound edition, famous for its photo of Jane Jacobs in a bar in Greenwich Village, with a cigarette in her hand. The photo was soon altered and the cigarette deleted.

We do not need to carry *Death and Life*, but it is what we do. And that is how you are perceived.

I wrote a small, specific book, *How to Wash the Dishes*, and have always hoped that it might become a classic. But that is a very difficult status to achieve.

The book must make friends; it must have a good appearance and an appropriate one, it must sit in time, and as time changes, and it must have a good feel, a good title, and a good length fitting to its subject.

The decision, of course, will be made by the people, over the same kind of time that makes sharp rocks smooth. I know that *Dishes* has fine qualities; I know that its design is subtle, and inspired; I know that it will teach many people how to literally do the dishes. I do not know if it can or will be a classic—but I do hope so.

Years ago, on an exploratory trip to Copenhagen, we took the train up the Whiskey Belt to the remarkable Louisiana Museum of Modern Art. It is twenty-five miles or so up the coast from Copenhagen, en route to Hamlet's castle at Elsinore.

The Louisiana may well be the most elegant contemporary art museum in the world. It was created by

Knud Jensen, and named to honor the original owner of the house, who had three wives who were all named Louise. It may also, of course, be the museum least known in America—many people have looked for it in Louisiana.

It is a brilliant place. We spent a wonderful day there, viewing the current exhibition on the wonderful Danish designer Poul Kjærholm. It is not a simple task to make an exhibit of furniture fascinating. Somehow, the Louisiana handled the task with ease. Everyone should go.

Walking back to town to catch the train, we arrived moments too late and watched the back of the last train car disappear up the tracks. A gentleman was just getting to his automobile and laughed, "Hah, you have missed the train! Come, I will give you a lift to the next station." We all climbed in.

It turned out that Carsten worked for a design company that I knew, Ørskov—their headquarters were nearby, in Klampenborg, so we took a visit. They are famous for their set of poster hangers, thin aluminum rods with a slot along their length that allows any size poster or print to be hung, gracefully. The MoMA gift shop certainly has sold millions of these poster hangers.

But he showed us their lovely glassware, in eight varying sizes, made from borosilicate glass. Each glass is

uniformly thin; you can feel their difference. By design, they can hold very hot or very cold liquids. They are perfectly Danish. I had never thought to carry glassware, but these were glasses that I wanted and that was enough review for me.

We have sold them now for twenty-five years, to singles and to couples, for weddings and for fundraisers. We have served soup in them and iced tea, yogurt, and wine. As the Graham Foundation in Chicago noted after a large benefit dinner, "People love them and notice them and at the end of the dinner, sometimes they take their glass with them. Who takes the glass from their dinner party? We need replacements."

Of course, when you sell glassware, other things come to mind. Soon, you are looking at spoons, and other glasses, and, oddly enough for me, dish towels. Such is retail—you tell it, it tells you.

Certain Days

One fall day, a gentleman came in and slowly walked about the shop. He said, "I am from Japan, and this is a most wonderful shop. I would like you to help me with my library. I would like one of every book that you sell and every book that you know about design."

You never imagine hearing such a request. I asked, "But do you want all of the books, and do you want us to ship them to Japan?"

"Yes," he said. "That is what I want. That would be wonderful."

We made arrangements with his office in Japan. It was very exciting and a compliment and saved us for the whole of what was a difficult year. I called every publisher that I knew and said, for the first and only time, I need you to send me one of every design book that you have.

The greatest difficulty was alphabetizing. This was well before computers, so we made alphabetical stacks of books, A to Z. There were all of the books from the shop, and the boxes of books coming now each day and then being repackaged for the trip to Japan.

In all, it took three months to complete the order. I was very proud to have been consulted and proud that we had begun a new design library, at a new design school in Nagasaki. We were something, and something is always a great help.

A shopkeeper puts on essentially the very same show each day. It is always *Oklahoma!*—and it is good fortune if you like the music and are cheered each time you see the show. And even greater fortune if people come for the show.

— 5 —

SEEING TIME

We have always had a wall clock, a fine Arne Jacobsen City Hall version: white face, black lines, twenty-nine centimeters. We have always set it where it could be seen from outside the shop. A kind of public time.

We did not realize how much work the clock was doing—until we moved it. Suddenly, there were notes under the door: *Put the clock back*. As they walked by, people counted on knowing what the time was. It was their time.

We have sold the Jacobsen City Hall clock for thirty years. Not in great quantity, but regularly. The Nordstrom offices consider it a staple of their interior design. One fall, they called and asked if we had one in stock—we did, and someone came over for it within minutes. Apparently, the City Hall clock sat just outside the executive office elevator. Someone had taken the clock right off the wall, leaving only the faded shadow where it had been. They needed that space repaired, immediately.

The clock also sits in the director's office of the San Francisco Giants. The managing director had called me at my son's soccer game and asked what was the perfect wall clock for their new office. City Hall, I said, City Hall, that is the one.

People Come

One Thursday afternoon, in the November dark, a man came in wearing a long black overcoat and walked slowly to the far corner of the shop. He did not look up nor say a single word.

We play recorded music all day. At that moment, a new CD of jazz selections from the 1920s was just starting. Three or four notes played, a saxophone, and the man looked up, at the speaker high on the bookcase, and said "Bechet." I looked at the liner notes of the CD and, of course, it was Sidney Bechet on saxophone, a recording in Paris, 1925.

He was pleased to hear Bechet. And out he went, never a word, other than *Bechet*.

Passing the Time

You never want to wait. As a shopkeeper, you never want the position where you can only wait. You want the job to be like any job, with things to do, a day full of things to do. You have invented the job, you have invented the culture, and part of your task is to fill that day, to make the job a part of the parade of a day.

You may have too much to do. Too many boxes have arrived, too many things need to be inventoried and arranged and entered. But, as a shopkeeper, you quietly have a further task—you must sell something.

For many people, that is not a part of their tasks; they simply have things to do and shall do them all day. They shall catch up, move ahead, or fall behind. But for a retailer, there are different factors, different tides, and different intuitions. The basics remain constant but there is the unusual factor of hoping and trying to sell things.

You cannot simply wave your hands. I do recall, with the greatest humor, the wonderful clothing shop that was my neighbor on First Avenue. It was a very hip shop, certainly hipper than we were. But at times, there would be slow periods. A factor of who only knew what, perhaps humidity, perhaps economy, perhaps the moon, perhaps the stars. The deepest fear, of course— never directly spoken—would be that the inventory, the theater of it, was no longer the hippest, a change that could indeed happen in a single season.

Whatever the case, they did have one very quick solution. The two sales directors were both remarkably attractive and completely brave: they would simply dress up in the craziest outfits, put a small table and two chairs outside on the sidewalk in front of their shop, and go sit out there. And talk, and laugh. It worked, every time. People would come, and moments later, everyone would be part of the café of shopping.

Design Research, the wonderful design-centric European-housewares shop in the 1960s and '70s, had a similar technique. They represented the brilliant Finnish clothing and textile company Marimekko. In Finland, there are full days of sun in summer and days of no sun in winter. Marimekko fabric was a literal antidote to the winter and high praise to the summer—bright, full colored, large patterns. No one in the world was making any fabric that was more obviously fun than Marimekko.

Design Research was the only company in the States importing Marimekko. On certain days, the entire import staff from Finland, twelve young women sent to represent the line, would dress up in the newest designs and bustle out into Harvard Square. A kind of mobile pop along fashion show. Suddenly, the shop, two blocks away, would be filled with customers and lookers.

It is not always possible to be, or to imagine how to be, so public. Instead, you must work in place, internally. Sometimes, at slow moments, we would take the entire center display apart, hundreds of pieces, right in the center of the day. Clean everything, dust and clean and polish. Then, we would reconsider what pieces should be featured. And which should be reassigned. The deeper you cleaned, the deeper you deconstructed, somehow it would be and feel like a revival.

There is an old saying: If you want the phone to ring, climb up on a long ladder without the phone.

There is another old saying: It is easy enough to be a retailer when you are busy. The true retailer will find a way to be busy when there is nothing going on.

Most importantly, it is your spirit, your invention, your imagination that must be kept as active and fresh as possible. It is your workplace—you must commit all that you possibly can so that it does not feel stale. To you or to anyone else.

In retail, nothing runs in a straight line.

Once Upon

I ate in this Italian luncheon café a hundred times and can easily tell as many stories. It was at an odd junction of streets, so it was hard to find if you did not know. Everyone shared the tables—often, we would wait until nearly two o'clock in the afternoon to meet for lunch. There was more room and even a little more wine.

Slowly, because it was so good, it became very popular and harder and harder to get into. And then it closed. And moved, to a more public location. There is no sign, not a single one, of what the original location was like, what fun and friendship it held. The breath is gone.

A Terrible Location

There is a true reward should you solve a terrible location. In a sense, the High Line in New York City is perhaps the

most brilliant poster of a transformed terrible location. Once an abandoned, miles-long steel trestle, it is now part of the true theater of Manhattan.

If you create life in a terrible location, then that location contributes a very special, and soulful, spirit, a kind of difficult reward. Much of New York's soul was saved by creating the High Line. Some of that rescue has been sadly lost to decisions of tourism and new privacy on the current High Line. But even now, when you walk that trestle, at certain times and certain stretches, you feel how great it is, the power of its rescue.

Forty years ago, in Seattle, a coffee shop named Raison d'Être opened just off First Avenue, on Virginia Street. The times were lean, and retail seemed possible only in two-dimensional locations and certainly not on side streets.

But Raison d'Être was very specific and very special and very actual. The coffee was superb, no one asked *For here or to go, single or a double?* and the brioche was big and sexy, as were the butter and the jam. They had four kinds of jam and two baristas who would become original Pearl Jam musicians.

It was an instant success; we all went and its terrible location became its privacy, its intimacy, and its nature. And suddenly, everyone knew where it was. The strength of character and imperfection.

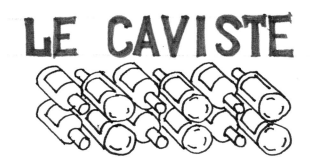

LE CAVISTE

When a shop succeeds in a terrible location, the very neighborhood is rewarded. The boundaries of space are widened; the streetscape says yes, instead of appearing mute or even sullen.

There is a Seattle wine bar, Le Caviste, that opened ten years ago in what was a terrible location. It is just west of the birch trees at the US District Courthouse, but few know the building or the trees. And for complicated, often perverse reasons, no one used that street section to walk on. It was the backside of a drive-in movie theater. Pedestrians simply used other streets.

A strictly French wine bar is not for everyone, but Le Caviste has literally brought its block to life. The people who walk by are quietly cheered by the life of it—and this little spur of a street is now a busy little spur.

Street Tales

I have a good friend from the book industry who sends us children's books, new and sample editions. Our children's section is very small and very particular and most of the new books did not fit there.

I would take many of the books home. My kids were little, and it was a luxury to have books all over the floor and table.

A local bakery truck stopped each morning to deliver baguettes across the street at the French restaurant. They were the best baguettes in the city. I asked their office if we could buy a couple each day for our lunch, but the logistics did not work.

I asked the driver if they ever had any extra? And a few days later, he came in with two. He would not take any money but I asked, do you have young children? With a big smile, he said he had three little ones. We gave him a good stack of children's books.

He would come by a couple times each week with two baguettes. And get a bunch of books. He said his kids loved them, and his wife loved them.

I would also take a stack to our pediatrician's office and leave them in the waiting room.

In those days, the shop was located on a very busy First Avenue. For some reason, the street signs were not clear that you could not park there from 3:00 to

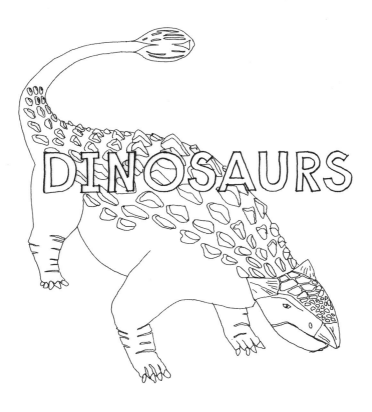

DINOSAURS

6:oo p.m. every weekday afternoon. And every afternoon, cars would be towed away.

As a shopkeeper, you have a quiet, unspoken responsibility to your literal section of the street. You keep quiet track of it and help, however you can.

One afternoon, a family from east of the mountains came into the shop, in obvious great distress. They did not know that their car, and three others, had been towed. To their three children, it had been stolen, by crazed forces, with all of their stuff, and all was hopeless and lost in a strange city.

We gave each of the kids a stack of new, unopened children's books. It worked, as miracles work. They sat on the floor with their books.

We got a very long, sweet thank-you note from the parents a week later, signed by each of the kids.

"

As a shopkeeper,
you have a quiet,
unspoken responsibility
to your literal section
of the street.
You keep quiet track
of it and help,
however you can.

"

— 6 —

THE NATURE OF SPACE — DOG ON A PORCH

A million things happen when your customer enters the shop. They notice the temperature, the smell, the feel of the floor or carpet, the sound, the depth and the height, the air itself. They notice if there is complexity, if there is privacy, if they are invited further or kept in waiting. They notice if you are on the phone.

As a shopkeeper, you must account for conditions. What do you want? Do you want the customer to feel cautioned, as you might if you sell glassware, or bold, as you might if you sell athletic equipment?

Do you want them to feel independent, protected, and adventurous, or timid and hesitant and eager to ask for help? Is it your hope that they will touch and open things or your dream that they will simply look and pause? There was a famous Manhattan design shop that sold mousepads that said *Do Not Touch*, and they meant it. They did not want anyone to touch anything.

It is not completely a matter of control—but it is a distinct matter of intent. A thicker carpet will surely slow a space, as might shading or a longer wall of gray color or an adagio from the Italian composer Albinoni.

We inherited, years ago, a lovely shop that had been designed for an art museum. It was beautifully detailed and constructed, with elegant maple casework and shelving and extraordinary steel windows. But it

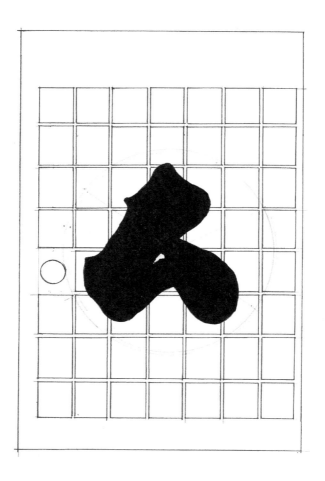

did not work and had not worked. They had asked if we would try to make it work.

The shop was within the museum but it had a perfect view to the south, out toward Mount Rainier. The sales counter faced north, so any customers could look out to the south, to where most of the weather began. It was indeed a lovely view, but that was not helping the shop.

We moved the counter precisely to the north side. It took considerable persuasion. The detailing was intricate and the move expensive—but it made all the difference. Now, the customer would pay attention to the shelves behind the counter, to the books that were on display, to the products in the case, even to the salesperson. Books and exhibition catalogs have for the most part a pacifist's soul—they cannot compete with loud sounds, bells, or whistles, or even landscape.

The staff, as well, loved the move of the counter. Now they could see and greet people as they came in. And, if there was a moment to pause, they had the hills and the landscape for their pause.

Matters of space and intuition are difficult to arrange and control. There is a new museum bookshop in New York City that bravely presented their book selection directly at the front of their space.

But it did not work. To look at the books, the customers had to put themselves in public view of the front window—an exhilaration for a moment, but books rely on and need a different privacy than that. It made some sense, but it was not helpful.

Cups and Surfaces

The very first Starbucks shop is in the Pike Place Market. It is not literally the first location, but it is very close.

Today there are long lines of tourists, waiting to visit and to shop in the very first location.

The shop was designed by the brilliant George Suyama. It is great fun, this first shop. They had the first coffee grinders and espresso machines ever displayed in America.

It is a basic L-shaped design—the long stem of the L was the counter on the right and the base stepped left at the back. The counter itself was a beautiful piece of wood, oiled and stained to a perfect hue, satin and partly reflective.

The counter composed the shop. It was the order, the grace, the nature, and, in a way, the point of the shop. It had a lovely, singular length.

At first, the counter was kept completely clear, from one end to the other and across the back. But slowly, merchandise began to appear on the counter. And to sell itself, for it was a very special stage.

The designers pointed out that the counter was not meant for display; its task was to set, specifically, the sense of the shop. It was a distinct reference to forest, to farming, to surface, to coffee plantations, to rendition.

At times, the counter would be cleared. But inevitably, merchandise would find a way back.

When Starbucks was sold, the wavering ended. The counter became a place of display, from one end to the other.

Even today, thirty years later, I look into the shop and think how lovely it would be if the counters were still in their first edition.

Obviously, the merchandise on the counter sells well. Less obviously, the sense of the shop is not as clear. A clear sense is intoxicating, and has its own value and allure.

The Ten Best

A gentleman came in, in a kind of hurry, but with some humor about his rushing. "What a shop," he said, pointing up to the high shelves. "What a shop! Okay, let's do it. Sell me the ten best books on architecture, the ten best."

I laughed and said, "It is like wine, I will sell you the ten most expensive books in the shop." "Yeah," he said, "that is what I want, the ten best."

So I went up to the highest shelves and brought down the most expensive books we had. The twelve volumes of the Frank Lloyd Wright collection, $4800. The three-volume set of Alvar Aalto's complete works, $350, and the complete eight volumes of Corbusier, $975; the nearly complete Palladio, two out-of-print Louis Kahns, two beautiful Neutras. A big, long, heavy stack of books. There were, in all, nine items. (To be honest, I was a little sorry to see some of them go.)

For the tenth book, I added the wonderful Tanizaki essay *In Praise of Shadows*, a very slim paperback book that says clearly on the back "$9.95." He laughed and said, "I asked for the ten best books, with no limits, and you sell me a book for $9.95?"

I said, "Well, it is one of the ten best." He said, "Fine, make it eleven then." I went back up to the high shelves and brought down the elegant Electa slipcase volume *Filippo Brunelleschi: The Complete Work*. He was thrilled.

Light

Any shop must address a great list of details, but the list, and the answers, may be more intuitive than fundamental. They may even change with time, or within time, as the seasons alter the space.

We had three large picture windows at the front of our bookshop. They posed significantly different problems

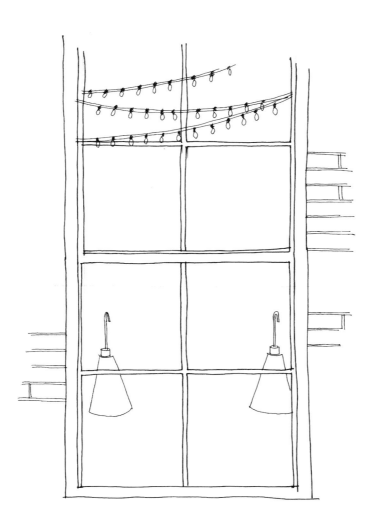

in the winter than in the summer. In summer, we needed to control the heat gain from the western exposure. That was simple enough until we discovered that the shading left us appearing more closed and similar to a mortuary than a design shop would hope for. And there was already a mortuary on the other side of the street.

In the winter, the flat gray light gave us a lifeless appearance, especially from across the street. Our afternoons seemed unusually quiet. By adding a very plain Italian desk lamp with a sixty-watt incandescent bulb, we looked suddenly quite alluring. And open.

How Do You Look

A good shop takes its direction from the existing space—where is the natural light, how does it change, what will it affect? You may decide to block the view to the street, to create privacy and enclosure and give yourself a true stage for a shop window. That is the typical department store solution.

Or you may want to leave the window as a visual access into the store, declaring yourself in a most open and clear way. There are advantages to both solutions, but there are consequences as well.

You must go outside your shop and look at it—in every season and at many different times of the day. It is literally how you look and how you are perceived.

I know a kitchen shop that has blocked each of its windows with wire Metro shelving, stacked high with many products, pots and pans, and colanders. And you cannot see into the shop at all.

To me, the window display signals only clutter and even excess and reminds me of the worst parts of my own pots and pans beneath my counters. I am sadly reminded I must do some serious cleaning and not buy more things.

The shop is blessed with lovely light from the south. Let the light in on the collection of French pots and pans. I want to see into the space much more than I want to see a stack of inventory.

Something there is that doesn't love a wall—or a blocked window.

If you leave your display windows open, you face a harder task of display. We thought ourselves very clever by making an open display with some lower bookcases set back from the picture window. Anyone could walk up to the display case and reach the books that were on display.

It worked elegantly for a moment. But soon the customers had pulled out the new books, laid their coats across the top shelf, and left strollers parked every which way.

We solved the problem with a very low, symbolic, and nonstructural railing detail. It was only a very thin rod with a couple of upright pieces, but it worked perfectly.

It was a metaphor of a fence—a two-foot-high mock-up, a quarter-inch steel rod literally laid atop two upright chunks of wood. It was too thin and too low to put a coat on.

Shopkeeping is not a universal affection. Julia Child was a kind of shopkeeper, but Vladimir Putin is not. The Yankees would turn America into "a nation of shopkeepers." The Deep Southerners were "a race of statesmen, orators, military leaders and gentlemen." And distinctly not shopkeepers.

Albert Einstein was a kind of shopkeeper—and General Robert E. Lee was not.

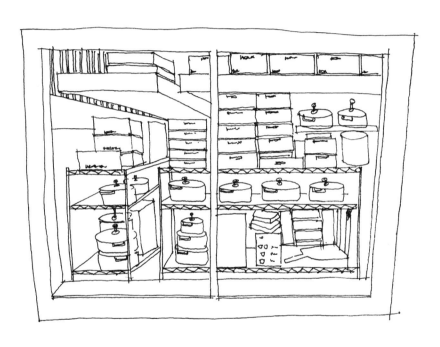

— 7 —

COUNTERS

The sales counter is a central figure in the play. It is the opening and ending to a visit to a shop. It may not at all be clear where it should be located. For many years, I insisted that the pieces that created the sales counter be on rollers—I wanted the option to move it completely. The shop had an L-shaped configuration and I could not determine which of six locations would prove to be the best. To make matters worse, I believed that one of the locations would prove to be not only the best but also correct, and true.

Over our twenty-eight-year residency there, we moved the counter to all six possibilities, often causing significant disruption and, as the computers became more sophisticated, chaos. Finally, on the very last move, I realized the answer. There was a lovely twenty-foot-high concrete wall behind the counter—I had never had the courage to park a counter in front of it, so proud was its effect.

The counter gave the wall stature. It became the area that we reserved for our finest books and objects. They looked handsome displayed in the casework against the wall—it was their best appearance. Each day, something would happen, or something would be noticed, or something would be sold that made it clear: the counter had found its proper place.

I told the story of the counter to the manager of a wine shop. He liked the story and even asked what I thought of their counter. I said the location seemed fine, but I wondered if he would consider changing the view that I had of the shelves behind him. Much of the time at a wine shop is spent at the counter, talking of wine, and all I could see from my side were stacks of invoices, three coffee cups, a pair of sneakers in a gym bag, and a charging iPhone.

Weeks later he came out as I was walking by and pulled me into the shop. Gone was the flotsam behind the counter, true as it might have been to the task of running a shop. Now there was a handsome display of Champagnes and four types of amaro, lovely wine glasses, and some very special dessert wines. And they had never sold as well before.

The sales counter is the first and last act of the play.

Two Salts

There is a famous food shop in Sydney, Australia, called Fratelli Fresh that bravely declares its preferences.

Rather than displaying hundreds of salts from around the world, they display only two varieties. And, if you ask them, they will patiently explain why they consider the two varieties to be the best they can offer. And to make their point as clear as possible, they have

2023 January

M	T	W	T	F	S	S
						1
2	3	4	5	6	7	8
9	10	11	12	13	14	15
16	17	18	19	20	21	22
23	24	25	26	27	28	29
30	31					

each variety in a single display, two hundred or so of each kind, carefully stacked.

They believe that their experience in selling and preparing food (they have a fine restaurant on the top floor) gives them a strong sense of what is the best product.

To their minds, that knowledge is valuable to their customer—they accept that their task is to choose the best salt. Interestingly, they sell many varieties of vinegar. For olive oil, they display only three types but in eight different sizes.

It is a very brave store, this one. You walk through a small, literal garage to the fruit, meat, and vegetable departments and then walk upstairs to the dry goods. And next to the dry goods is the wine selection. And next to the wine, they have a glassed-in restaurant that looks out to the street. It all makes perfect sense when you are there.

Time on Paper

It is a curious detail that we sell so many paper calendars. We have the most electronically sophisticated audience in the world.

They all use electronic calendars for planning and reminding and cross-referencing—yet they all buy paper calendars. They are not being sentimental or retro. In fact, they are a particularly ill-humored set—should their particular calendar be sold out, they take offense.

It is an interesting form, a calendar. It is a linear presentation of day and time. But that is just the bread and water of it—the details have long since been refined into subtleties that care not a whit if you notice them at first glance.

The calendar, and in particular the day planner, has an extraordinary intimacy to it—it is the underwear of time. You have it with you every day and if it does not fit, if it is too tight or too thick, if it is awkward or inanimate, if it does not suit you, then you are at odds, like wearing badly fitted underwear.

But if it does fit, if it is you, then all is smooth, and correctly intimate and a compliment and a comfort and a confidence. The Italians were the first to take more than a pure graphic interest in the calendar.

By the late 1960s, Nazareno Gabrielli and Nava Milano had created a new level of detailing and elegance for the modest calendar. They weighed the borders and the columns, the numbers and the lines, the dates and the spaces, and they literally designed a better form. No one had taken the daybook so seriously; no one had combined work and privacy, labor and pleasure, intent and daydream so subtly. When the calendars were released in the fall for the coming year, it was news, and all the shop windows had signs announcing that the new calendars had come.

The paper calendar is not in contest with the electronic calendar, any more than a cashmere sweater is competing with an undershirt. They share a task—they do not share emotions or textures or dreams. Or loyalties.

The very unpaperlike aspect of technology has fueled and fertilized an industry of note-taking, writing, and drawing.

The customers want very good paper, often the best paper, and they want a choice of grids, lines, and blanks. They plan to keep what they have sketched, written.

For both the calendar and the notebook, it is the literal entry of words and drawings that have created a passion. The touch of a pen or a pencil to a surface is the ignition. There is a physicality of muscle and brain and intuition and memory that exists only on this stage, on point.

The actual is being revived and restored by the digital.

Where Leads Will Lead

For many years, until the 1970s, the typical mechanical pencil used a 0.5 mm lead. There were several manufacturers—Koh-I-Noor, Faber-Castell, Lamy, Caran d'Ache, Parker—and the pencil of choice used the 0.5 mm size lead.

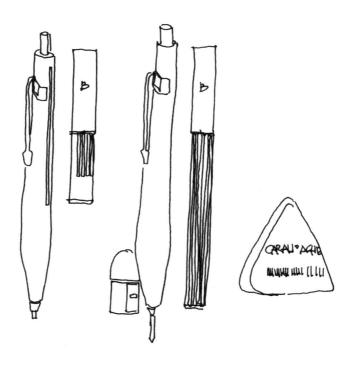

But the quality of the lead began to deteriorate. The lead became cheaper and less discriminate. In a way, it was similar to the light bulb, which also lost much of its distinct character by being mass produced. They followed in step with the BIC razor and fast food. And, some would say, education and spelling.

A few years ago, I asked the head of Caran d'Ache why his leads were literally twice as expensive as other leads. He said that when you make a pencil lead, you choose the graphite, from a ninety-nine percent pure quality down to sixty percent pure graphite. Like coal, the better graphite is more expensive. And the sand that they use to bind the lead, they purchase from Africa. Also expensive. But, he noted, the lead is superior. It has a finer, more even touch. You can tell the difference by using it, if you pay attention, but you cannot tell the difference by appearance.

Most importantly, it is not fragile; it does not break. In the 1970s, the 0.5 mm lead, now produced as inexpensively as possible, began to break, like a poorly made matchstick. And each person blamed themselves—they were obviously using too heavy a hand. Instead of blaming the lead, they blamed themselves, quietly.

The solution was simple: use a larger lead, a 0.7 mm—that one will not break. Almost suddenly, the 0.5 mm mechanical pencil, the very standard bearer, became near obsolete. Everyone went for the larger size lead and that took care of the lead breaking. The 0.5 mm became the fading relic. And by the 1980s and '90s, there were virtually no mechanical pencils in the 0.5 mm range. Even Caran d'Ache, the stubbornest of Swiss manufacturers, changed their most famous pencil to the 0.7 mm size. They literally stopped making the 0.5 mm. The customer had moved on.

There are, of course, people who still use and intend to use a 0.5 mm mechanical pencil. Lamy still offers both sizes in their more expensive line. But you must keep track of which size you are using. If you should refill your pencil with a larger lead, or perhaps a less precise lead, then your pencil will clog with the fatter lead.

It was once a tradition that the eraser of a good mechanical pencil would also have, on its interior end, a filament that was precisely the width of the pencil lead size. If your mechanical pencil was failing to advance the next lead, then you could use the filament to clear the barrel, so to speak. If you did not have such a filament, then you were out of luck. Your pencil was stuck. The tolerances are precise.

Needless to say, the migration to the larger 0.7 mm lead created a much bigger caseload of jammed pencils.

Miracles and Spirits

It will be a miracle if your shop succeeds. But you cannot have the miracle unless you open. And then you have the chance.

There were times in the 1980s that were very difficult—really, they were impossible. I used to say, had I been a Broadway show, I would have closed in a week. Or a fortnight. But I was a shop, with fixtures and inventory. You push on. And hope. And try not to look.

I came in one morning and the staff said that someone had called—they had architecture books to sell. I called them, with little expectation, for the days had been very slow and that can quietly wear out your expectations. They explained that they were in Anacortes, about one and a half hours north, and these were books from their father.

By a coincidence, I had talked that morning to the local Saab dealer. They suggested that I try a Saab for a day. Off I went to Anacortes, in a lovely auto. (Later, they easily sold me a one-year-old Saab sedan, a car I still miss.)

The house was in a midcentury suburb of the seaside town. They had laid all of the books out in the basement rec room, on folding tables. They then explained that their father had been the librarian at the UC Berkeley

Department of Architecture in the 1930s, and this was his own collection.

I will never see such a collection again. Everyone was there, every great and brilliant and famous architecture book from the '20s and '30s, from New York and Los Angeles and Chicago, from London and Berlin and Paris and Rome. Stanford White was with Piranesi, Frank Lloyd Wright was with Schinkel, Mendelsohn was with Ponti. There were portfolios and collections, and, for a moment, in a basement, no one was more starstruck and thrilled than I. I could barely move from book to book, so powerful was their effect.

They were thrilled to see my enchantment. I wish, of course, that I could have bought them all. I bought what I could. As I drove back to the shop, the Saab filled with boxes, I could barely think of anything else.

I arrived after closing time and loaded the boxes into the back office. I sat and looked at the boxes and finally reached for the top book, *Sketches and Designs by Stanford White*, a book I had always heard about, but had never seen nor touched.

I laid it flat on my wide desk and sat and opened it. And something, I shall never, of course, know what, flew out, poof, up into the high corner of the office ceiling, poof, gone. What a day, what a collection of books.

Years later, Steven Holl, the wonderful architect born in Puget Sound, would buy one of the books—the famous *Recueil et Parallele des Edifices de Tout Genre Anciens et Modernes, J.N.L. Durand* from 1801, the original one with ninety-one plates. As he looked at it, and felt the pages, he noticed the signature at the front: *Amitié, J.N.L. Durand.*

No one has better defended and supported this shop—and the brilliant William Stout Architectural Books in San Francisco—than Steven Holl. He has sent his own watercolor drawings when we needed to raise money for a project. He has signed books for hours. I was pleased the Durand was with his own library. A long journey from Paris.

— 8 —

TO MOVE

Sometimes, you have to move. To look for a new space that will suit your shop is a terrible task. The rent has forced your hand, or the building has been sold, or the neighborhood has changed, or you are restless.

You have the details of your shop, a history of too few windows or too many, of noise and pollution, of security and prospects. You go forth and look at new spaces.

You know, for certain, that whatever space you might choose, you will change it and it will change you. You will become part of a fabric that you do not yet know. You have hopes and experience. But you are, for the moment, the newcomer.

Your shop may be just the thing. The spark and the intuition that will make the street come alive. I have always felt hopeful. But there are places that do not work. And the reasons can be hard to know.

I asked a good customer how he liked our new space. He paused and then said, I love your shop. But the walk to it, from any direction, is depressing.

Our last move was six years ago. I decided I had been too narrow-minded and must now consider new districts, new formats, and perhaps even a new city. I did not, of course, know that a plague was coming.

I tried a hundred locations, most of them in my thoughts only. I brought a chair to several locations, and sat outside them in the early evening to see who walked by, who was there when the day was ending.

In my mind, I moved to Portland, for Portland loves narrow streets and specific retail. And to Vancouver, for they have some wonderful streets and a deep tradition for honoring retail. They love shops.

I moved closer to the Seattle Art Museum, realizing that it would be a very good wagon train for a small shop like mine and others. I moved up to Capitol Hill, for they have a wonderful tradition of people being out on the streets in the evenings.

I called several of my best friends and asked their advice. In the end, after feeling as if I were speed dating, I chose a location in an alley, behind a mission, that had never been a retail site. It was the oddest of all the choices, but it had some unique, handsome details.

For the first time in my life as a retailer, when I looked out the storefront windows, I was looking not at traffic but at a lovely 125-year-old brick exterior wall. The bricks are a dozen different shades of color, some even black. No one imagined that the bricks themselves, now sandblasted, would ever be on public display.

Looking for a new retail space is like going clothes shopping, but with no particular size in mind.

Smaller and narrower, you imagine, *Well, this might work!* Bigger and wider, you think, *Hah, perhaps I have been too small and narrow!*

Language of a Shop

How is your day going so far?

Who started this? How long ago? Has it been a few years or much more than that? This business of asking your customer contrived questions, as if that were cunning, or fair, or even decent.

I sat the staff down and said, no more, we are not asking anyone anymore, *Would you like a bag?* Enough of these questions, they are a tic, and a poke, and a poker, and all they signal is that you did not look and think at all, you just jabbered away.

Look at the customer, at what they bought, and what they think, and the weather and the date and their hands and their friends and their attitude. It will take but a moment. If they need more, or less, then help. But asking, that is not helping.

*Would you like a single or a double—For here or to go—*it is the machinery of commerce but not of humanity. It is a misuse of language. And makes the interaction a token. *The task of a shop is to make the street and the time come alive, not to fall into a metronome of smiley-faced hellos.*

— 9 —

THE ELECTRONICS
OF IT

I was slow to realize that my customers liked getting notes. Not ad campaigns, not broad targets, but notes—details, that this came, that this was particularly good, that these work well.

They would like a note. To send such a thing, you will need their name and email address and probably phone number. It takes a bit of doing and attention—when someone comes by and purchases precisely what the shop is best at, then I want their address. I want to be able to send them a note; they are what we are.

You will need a small website that can show precisely what you have. What colors, what sorts, what series. One day, they will figure literally how to reenact a shop—not virtually but literally—and that will help your customer stay close to how it feels.

The text is important. Obviously, it should not be a version of the how-is-your-day-going-so-far tune. In a way, I have only one specification—we must not use contractions. They were made to reenact speech, to simulate the shorthand of talking.

But I favor the longhand and, in a sense, that is what a shop is, the longhand.

In the best world, the emails and the website reenact the shop. The sense of one is the sense of the other.

Posts, Email, or Other

We do our email posts as a kind of hors d'oeuvres tray.

Sometimes there are olives, often hummus and feta— with luck, chives, some basil, cherry tomatoes, sometimes beets and last night's roasted red potatoes, pickled red onions, lentils that we nearly forgot, and always lemon and olive oil. On the corner, we add a small stack of naan or pita that we heat, cut into wedges, and toss with salt and olive oil, to pick up the parts.

We show in our posts what is new, we let parts play together, and we put on a moment's vignette. It is a kind of hand-painted postcard of the shop. Wish you were here.

When the customers start to look forward to the posts, when they say *These are one of the few things we read in our inbox*, then you are on the right trail.

You have, in a way, two clients. You have the people who will read the post. They are your customers and —they get a lot of mail—you will do best if you protect them from boredom, poor grammar, and halfhearted spirits.

And you, you are also a client—the post must interest you, it must involve you.

It is a great deal like cooking.

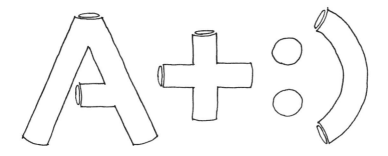

Electronic Issues and Repair

The internet creates some interesting and involved situations, and they can require some interesting and involved solutions. For nearly a year, we received emails and phone calls from customers all over the country who were frustrated that their orders or returns were not being processed.

Hi, I am having trouble using my gift certificate!

You want to solve these things. They are the courtesy requisite to all good commerce.

In the majority of cases, it turned out that the difficulty involved a clothing company titled Peter Millar, a company that had carefully positioned itself to show up first online, if you were even close to its name.

For various absurd reasons, we began to get a small chunk of their frustrated customers. People would call, wondering where the hell their chinos and sport shirts were, or what had happened to their returns credit.

We answer the phone ourselves. Most of the customers would call—not in the best mood—but it took only a minute to explain that we were not a clothing company and we were spelled differently. We would always add that if we had the shirt or the product, we would have certainly sent it, pronto.

One customer said he had won a big gift certificate at a golf tournament, and our website was not allowing him to use it. I explained the problem to him, and he laughed, and said, I do not need any more shirts, but I want some of these books and pens, and that LED light that you show. He used his Amex card and considered it all an adventure in the metaverse.

Inventory

When the walls are painted, the shelves and counters installed, the lighting arranged, the signage in place, the floors finished, the bags and wrapping paper prepped, then a shop is ready to receive and present its inventory.

Inventory has three masters. It must please the owner, represent the product, and attract the customer. Every shop is defined by its inventory. Every shop is curated. The physical shop is the theater, the inventory is the play, and the interaction is the drama.

The owner is the curator, and will, consciously or not, decide how to choose each product. Should one trust implicitly one's own intuition, or trust the supplier, or listen to the customer? Typically, it is a bit of each counsel.

You must listen well, you must learn, and you must trust your intuition, a little. The best shops are always the most rigorous.

The public does not need you to show and stock the breadth of every salt or toilet paper in the world. It does need your sense of which salt and toilet paper might be the best.

It is a matter of selection.

Some shops do not realize that they cannot simply be good horizontally—they must also have moments and details that are vertical. You can sell six butters that are mostly the same, but you need a seventh butter that is something.

We carry some expensive leather briefcases that are made in Italy. They are lovely and more elegant, in certain ways, than other briefcases we might carry. They are not as durable as a JanSport bag, but the Italians do not want to carry around as much as the JanSport will carry.

One year, we ordered six black briefcases, two red briefcases, and one yellow briefcase. The yellow one was very bright and, to my mind, I could not imagine who would buy such a color. It was almost too brave.

But it did sell, one Christmas, about five years ago. And every fall, we receive an email and photo from its owner, showing where the bag is now.

There was an interesting interview with Chiara Alessi, the granddaughter of the founder of Alessi, the one-hundred-year-old Italian design products company:

> I am not a historian and I do not consider
> myself a curator. I come from a family of what
> some call shop owners.
>
> Perhaps my DNA is more entrepreneurial
> than curatorial or is curatorial in the way
> shopkeepers are.

In a Sense

Making orange juice is like shopkeeping. You have to take the long way. And you have to choose.

Which oranges shall I buy? There are four varieties offered, of varying sizes. The least attractive are the so-called juice oranges. But they often turn out to be the best.

What is the season? Intuitively, it would be summer for the best oranges, but here in the Northwest, the best oranges, from California and Florida, come in the late fall and winter.

Who am I making the juice for? Will they want an exquisite small glass of juice, by itself, or a larger twelve-ounce glass, perhaps with ice?

I must carry the oranges back to the kitchen. I have the electric juicer but there is also the small juice strainer. It will depend on how many oranges I bring and how many people want juice. The juicer is quicker and easier for multiples, but the strainer is much easier to clean and store.

There are, of course, many ways to get a glass of orange juice—ways that do not involve lugging oranges, or squeezing, or cleaning up. There are more economical ways and less stringent ways.

In the end, it is the glass of juice that matters. If it is perfectly sweet and cool, and as fresh as possible, if it is in the proper glass, then nothing else could be better. You have done the work, the research, and the production.

There are times when the shop is very good. There are times when the shop is only fair. And there are certain times when the shop is superb. In that sense, the shop is indeed like a vegetable stand. At the moments when the vegetables and fruits are superb, then the stand shall also be superb.

The Big Shops

Walmart is a shop and Costco is a shop and Tiffany is a shop and Peter Miller is a shop. Each is a stage and each signals thousands of things, pheromones of sense and desire, mathematics and instinct.

Walmart wants to signal savings but it wants more than that—it wants to signal a time of leanness, when economy was a virtue and a fact and a courage. The very graphics of Walmart signal savings. They want to reenact the 1950s, Main Street, when there was simply no money for excess.

Costco comes in from a different slant. Costco promises a different time. Costco is the enactment of a privilege, alluded to in the Woody Allen line that the only sin in his family was buying something at retail.

In the 1950s, in much of the Western world, there was a separation of wholesale and retail—there was literally no place that you could go to purchase anything at a constant sale price. It was a firm and confirmed separation. It was like the Wild West, when horse rustling, stealing someone's horse, was a crime punishable on the spot by death. They needed people to not be able to steal horses or the whole fabric went south.

After World War II, America needed new towns, new cities, and new commerce. There could only be expansion if there was some protection of the price of goods. Main Street needed shops and shops needed the confidence that their goods were not going to be undersold.

It was a code that worked pretty well. If there were moments of wholesale offloading, they tended to be outlaw moments, fell-off-the-truck back-door sales. No one could count on or plan for an alternate price.

But the implicit agreement of it all simply could not hold. Many factors—overproduction, global imports, a heartbreaking war in Vietnam, a dangerous economy— all combined to make the 1970s and '80s a time of profound and cruel self-interest. Cleverness was again a virtue and a signal of strength.

And suddenly there were 7-Elevens, slashing the price of a simple soda and open the whole night, for the whole week. There were factory outlets for immodest fashion in modest outlying towns—and Home Depot, taking on the entire by-hand enterprise of hardware stores, lumberyards, and machinery centers.

The current headquarters for Starbucks had once been a lovely seven-floor center for Sears. On the weekends, there was no room to park—everyone was there. There were no special sales, but there were wonderful, knowledgeable salespeople, for everything from washers to wood joints.

Costco arrived in 1983, with a perfectly subversive idea—you could become a member of a quasi guild and get wholesale prices all the time. Every single day you were allowed behind the lines, into the warehouse.

You could buy products as if you were the owner's relative. You could buy it at near the price he bought it at—you were a member. And he was a good guy. The most trustworthy decoration used simply boxes and pallets. Nothing to worry, nothing to spare.

It turns out, of course, that a lot of people had always wanted to be a member. They had heard the rumors and the stories and the whispers that if you knew just the right person, well, things could be gotten at a much better price. There was a club, however secretive, and they wanted to join. *Sign me up, I am all over wholesale.*

In a way, that is precisely what Costco wants you to see and feel when you go there. They want it to be the 1980s forever, when the center was loosed and someone finally broke completely through and made it a sale forever. Even if you go to Hawaii, way over there, why, you can still drive out to a warehouse and fill your rental car with stuff. You are a member.

Costco does not budge. It does nothing for the houses next to it or the neighborhood, at least in terms of interaction. It is for the people from the next neighborhood over, who do not have a warehouse plopped in its center and would never dream of having one. The design and location of a Costco must signal that not a dime was spent on frills. We are sparing so that you will save.

As Walmart signals savings, Costco signals cost—as Walmart signals a hard leanness, Costco signals a private excess with a sharp eye to price.

They are both murder to actual shops, especially right out of the chute. Suddenly, you could not find a hardware store or garden store or grocer or butcher. And if you did buy your soda locally, you only bought six cans and later bought twelve times that many at Costco. Toilet paper and toothpaste—suddenly you could have a lot of it, great armloads.

Tiffany, of course, is another bird entirely. Tiffany needs to signal that, however uncertain the news and the nightmares of war and nature and mortgage, the world is still a sturdy rock, and you would do well to add a bit of elegance to your place in it.

When you walk into a Tiffany shop, they want you to feel both safe and in a safe, the safest place to keep such things. What is a diamond but a remarkable flicker from the world's darkest mines, a light from the worst depth of no light? Any jewelry store is part temple, a muffle to quick movement and loud noise, a refuge from clanking time.

Now consider Peter Miller, a bookshop. For such an endangered sort, you would be tempted to design a shop in recollective fashion—either the darkness and density of a City Lights Bookstore or the drawing room elegance of a Rizzoli store.

You would hark back to the smoky Updike/William Carlos Williams 1950s or further back to the wood-paneled couture of the 1930s. In the 1950s, there was a sense that you might linger as a kind of rebellion—in the 1930s, you might linger because you were inclined to do so.

But I wanted a different sense—a strict present tense—a sense of space held in order by design. A present tense created by graphic design, by industrial design, and by architectural design. The shop must represent and must signal that it all matters, that all of its detail is intentional.

There is a sense of design into the corners of the bookcase, down the walls, across the business card.

It is hard to do—it is hard to not lean on the past for comfort and direction and correctness. It is difficult to trust and design the present.

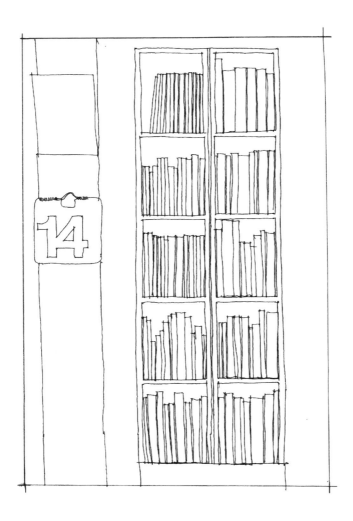

When we were imagining bookcases, I said I wanted them skinny, wry, and vertical—each cube no more than twelve inches wide. I did not want any customer cocking their head to read titles—I wanted them to look straight ahead. And to be proud of how the books looked, of how their shop looked.

We have always kept a particular affection, a passion, for lighting. When Artemide released the first Tolomeo lights, the perfect task lights, we added them to every corner. And one afternoon, the Artemide CEO pulled up in front of the shop in a rented limo. I had no idea who he was—he rushed in and asked, "How come you sell so many of my Tolomeos?" I laughed and said, "Because they are the best!" He flung his arms in the air, as if to say "See!" and left. I never saw him again, never spoke to him, but he made certain that I always had an Artemide account.

When Flos produced the first Mayday light, from the designer Konstantin Grcic, we brought the long cords together from a dozen of the lights, bound them like a braid, and set the Maydays in the middle of the floor.

And when Flos introduced the Bellhop, their rechargeable LED beauty, in all its colors, we ordered every color, with no hesitation. In a sense, it was like a gift to our customers, as if we had returned from a faraway place.

Lighting is like that—it is the most exciting modernism.

During one renovation, I had a crazy idea—it was never done, but I still believe in it. I wanted there to be rolls of light cotton fabric, twenty-four inches wide or so, above each case. Window shopping one early evening in Milan, I noticed a jewelry shop that seemed almost to have put their display cases to bed with long streams of cotton material that draped over each case. There were still pieces to see on display in the window— but the shop itself was resting.

I thought it would be perfect to see a bookshop and its books taking a rest. And then getting up in the morning.

A Very New Kind of Retail

Some shop spaces are now only open to advertise that they could be closed. Their strength is that they can be privately rented, as a space. To then be closed to the public but open as a special event. It is a new and intentional retail cleverness.

To look like what you once used to be but, in economic terms, to be something else entirely.

A shop is not an irony. It is a length. An actual, living part of the collective.

To Carry Radios

I wanted to carry a radio I had seen in Copenhagen. It was on prominent display in the wonderful Illums design store, in a dozen different colors. I had thought, naturally, that it was from Denmark. In fact, it was from a company in Cambridge, Massachusetts.

When I returned to the States, I contacted them, explaining my enthusiasm. But they had little interest in a shop carrying their radio—they had larger, big-boy distribution. The next year, returning to Copenhagen, I saw the radios again and was even more excited. And contacted the company again, and again they did not have any interest in smaller distribution.

In the third year, the electronics company contacted me, saying, with some humor, I bet you thought we would never call. I said no, that was not true, I simply thought you would get someone brighter. They laughed and said, so glad we called!

We made an arrangement. I said I wanted all the colors—they said all the colors were only sold in Europe. Ha! Well, bring them in, I suggested, the yellows and the pinks and such, this country is ready for colors. They did, and each time that I sold a bright yellow radio, I would email them. We became fine friends and soon they had located other design shops, museum shops in particular, and created a new market for the radios.

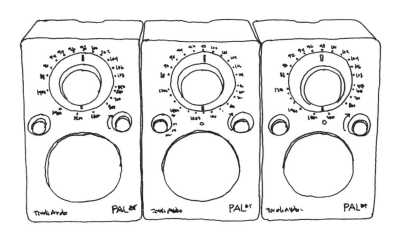

They did me a great favor—apparently, next to my account, there is a note that says *Send him whatever he wants*. There are times that it is impossible to get a certain color or a certain radio, but they always seem to find one for us.

(It is a special treat when the relationship to a vendor becomes personal, especially in a good way. I can remember precisely all of the suppliers from outside the United States who sent best wishes and hope to us right after the disaster of 9/11.)

Truth be told, I have only a partial interest in selling radios. But I love the look and design of these. And the customers are remarkably loyal to them.

We did have an issue one year. A person returned the radio. Apparently, by some quirk, it would make a garbled sound at night, even though it was turned off. It was spooky to them. They were very nice about it and loved the radio. I asked the company, in all seriousness, is there the most remote possibility of the radio making a sound when it is turned off, Bluetooth and all considered.

They took the question seriously, or pretended to, and answered no. It stayed a mystery for several months. Then, one day, the customer came back and sheepishly explained that their house had been remodeled. A smoke detector had mistakenly been buried in the bedroom wall. And that was the garbled sound, the detector asking for new batteries. They were thrilled to buy the radio again.

Locking the Door

One December 24th, years ago, in the early afternoon of a darkening day, after a busy week, it seemed there were no more Christmas shoppers left on the street.

Patrice, the half-French owner of the corner bar, came down to the bookshop and invited me to his bar for a holiday toast. My staff had, by then, all left for the day.

It is a comfort that, on Christmas Eve, people in the Market all seem to take a moment to get together—the fruit and vegetable families, the fish brokers, the shop owners, the stragglers. All were at the bar—some people had places they were supposed to be, and some were glad just to have a place to be. It is not raucous at the Virginia Inn, but it is very good-hearted and everyone can feel it.

On this occasion, several of us were bachelors, so we had to be careful to stay with the crowd or our singleness would start to not seem a great, or timely, decision. Christmas Eve is not the time you hope for a little time to yourself.

I did not get back to the shop for at least an hour and a half. Even then, it was only because Patrice wanted to close and asked me to join him at another event. It was dark, and very quiet.

We both walked down the block to the shop. There was no one around, and only a few cars parked on the street. But when we got to the shop, there were six customers in it, looking at books.

I had left half of the lights on and apparently had somehow forgotten to lock the front door. The customers simply wandered in, in ones and twos. We would not have been more surprised if there were ponies in the store.

Nothing was missing. I sheepishly walked through and took my position at the sales desk. People bought some books, everyone wished each other well. Later, Patrice opened a good bottle of champagne to tell the story about the look on both our faces.

I always think I have locked the door and always wonder if I have. Typically, I have to go back and check.

It is a help and true fortune if you still love your shop after thirty years—but some of that is not in your control. I have worked as hard on shops that failed as on shops that thrived.

"

A shop is not an irony.
It is a length.
An actual, living part
of the collective.

"

— 10 —

COMMERCE

Amazon was a setback to hands-on retail. It brought a kind of dishonor to the environment of a shop. Suddenly, time after time, people were asking for some help, then copying down the titles or products you had suggested, and then leaving without purchasing a single thing. They had not come to purchase; they had come to survey what they would later buy online.

The quiet sorrow was the tacky, stained edge that it put between the shopkeeper and the customer. It was impossible to not feel something. And it became clear that you needed to have caution as you dealt with your customers. "How may I help?" turned into a sadly complicated exercise.

Initially, Amazon was not even charging sales tax, a particularly ratlike ploy.

But time and honor and detail inexorably evened matters. The customers who only wanted the deal got over coming in. The customers who loved shops came more often. And some people learned to like and respect the quiet pulse of a shop. Each to their corner.

The shop learned to be hipper, smarter, quicker, and more specific. In a way, Amazon saved shops, pushing them to intents and accuracies they would never have needed.

I was amused when the discounters opened brick-and-mortar shops. I cannot, with a lance, take on the internet—but open next to me, and honestly, unless you have a hell of a heart and a good spirit, your cashier-less ways will look as natural as a military dictator trying to learn to salsa.

If you discount your goods, then you are a line cutter. And at many points in history, that was neither an honor nor a badge. Today, discounting may seem a subtlety, even a modernism or a necessary velocity. But it is always line cutting.

When You See a Shop

Walk into a McNally Jackson bookshop and every website in the world looks like a frozen rope. Walk into an Elliott Bay Book Company, and all you can see are books that you want to read. Walk into William Stout Architectural Books and you feel you are not current enough in design and late to class.

Walk into an Imperfetta wine shop and all you can think of is wine. Walk into a good bike shop and you want to ride. Walk into a fine food shop and you want to cook. Walk into Flora and Henri and you want to dress up. Walk into Edit., and you can only think of linen.

A true shop has a life, a breath, a status, set not by algorithms but by minds and hearts. And you know it.

What Are You

You are a showroom. A showroom of culture, a showroom of types and styles, a showroom of manners even, a lure of sorts but a quietly cinematic lure, hardly blaring or brazen. You are representing perhaps the present or the past or the future, or the present mixing of the three tenses.

You are luring the public into a show that typically does not move at all—it may twinkle a bit and even play music or flicker images, but that is barely the tinsel of it. No, the showroom is a subtler show than that—it is a show of what you could be or could have or could look like, what you might read, or should read, or did not even know anyone was reading. Or what you are reading and must read and will read.

A shop must confirm you. And poke you. And help you. And listen. And suggest and keep you company. Praise your attention and urge that you give more attention. It is, in part, a metaphor, a wonderful shoeshine, a bright intricate scarf, a new notepad, and six ideas that you did not have before.

It is a place that has what you have not seen, that has what you did not imagine, that has what you knew was true, that shows what you wanted and shows what you did not know.

A shop is a lure that you be more modern or less so, more careless or more subtle, more brave or more narrow. A good shop should make you feel correct or shrewd, wise or prudent, cautious or foolish, knowing or innocent.

It is a setting, in its very simplest form: a stage that you enter of your own will, and at its very best, you feel at home or feel it is the supplier of your stuff, the purveyor of how you want it to be or how you feel it must be. It may be a fantasy, it may even be fantastic, but it may also have the true air of being completely normal or completely plain. It may be many things, a shop, but it is always something—and if it tries to be no things at all, that, of course, is something.

When I was about ten years old, riding in the back seat, my mom driving, we passed a shop that had a sign, *Forty Percent Off*, and she said, ah, how sad. I did not understand what was sad. She said, they are nice people but their business is not working and they are closing.

It would never be that they were discounting to get ahead, to cut in line. There was no honor to that. They were simply going away.

The great discounters always vacation in Europe, so they can go somewhere that has shops and a streetscape.

Shops Today

It is an inventive, difficult time for new shops. A shop today must inform its customers but not barrage them—it must make the customer feel particular and fortunate. It simply must be good at precisely what it does. The world can get anything it wants. It cannot get a shop.

For a shop to survive, it must become part of the fabric of its customers, part of what they do, how they see themselves, and what they need. The shop affects how people travel, how they feel and think about a certain block. At its best, it civilizes space, space on the street. It is a yes, if only a tentative yes, to the length of the buildings and windows.

There is no literal need for shops. Certainly no need for ties, nor extra-virgin olive oil, nor a baguette; no need for notebooks from Italy and dot grid notepads from Tokyo; no need for Danish carafes and Swedish tea light holders; no need for hand-printed cards from Paris; no need to restock pencil leads and better pens; no need to compare sketchbooks, nor study Perriand, nor review the work of designer Paul Rand and his wife Ann; no need for the street signs of Paris, the graphics of Barcelona, the stone walls of Vals, no need.

But then, of course, "O, reason not the need." We shall as soon never cut flowers again, nor look to the night sky, nor walk in cool, shallow waters. Nor marvel, at the gifts of it all.

New Shops

There will be new shops, with wonderful new names like Cult Gaia and Imbroglio, World Enough and Time, Grayhorse and Canoe, To Be or Not and Perhaps. It is the nature of the human spirit. To match raspberries and fresh cream. To make better candlesticks and a clearer light. And a brighter day. To be something.

They will come from big towns and little towns, with equal imagination and inspiration. I remember perfectly the knife shop in Bozeman, on Main Street. Each sharp blade of the lovely handmade knives was nestled in a bed of dried beans, for looks and for safety.

To serve a book, a pat of butter, a bread knife, or a blouse, with a new eye.

Times Square

On a walking safari years ago in Zimbabwe, we ventured deep into the woods, ten of us with a guide, for several hours. As we walked deeper and deeper into the forest, it became less obvious where we were.

But then, we came upon a very large rock outcropping, twenty meters high in some places and probably eighty meters in length, a great, smooth lava-formed mass.

Each ledge, each pocket, indeed each distinction had a name, and even a legend, out there in the deepest woods. Our guide Justin explained many of the details—this was for the shaman, this was a stopping place for a medical doctor, this was a meeting center, this space was a kind of fresh vegetable stand, and one corner was where people met, to smoke and drink together.

It was Times Square in the woods. It was all a kind of retail. Good company, things to do, a sense of place.

Shopkeeping Aside / Last Notes

My father was a retailer. He ran a fine clothing shop in Hartford for thirty-three years; paid the considerable expenses of three children, two houses, ski vacations, buying trips to Europe, two good cars, and some golf; and retired to Florida.

He wrote notes about a first meeting with Ralph Lauren (the new wide ties made both his wife and daughter laugh out loud), about his two tailors cooking pigeon in the back room, about Count Basie becoming a careful customer.

He told stories of feeling like a country bumpkin in the fashion shops of Europe, of learning about truffles, of learning to trust the wonderful new colors and lines of European design.

In the end, though, it was golf that lured him the most, golf that challenged and thrilled him, golf that hired him as a skinny nine-year-old kid to carry two bags. He wanted to write a book titled *The Tropic of Golf*.

He taught me about shopkeeping. I was a terrible salesperson, working in his clothing shop. I had not one single idea what someone might or should want to wear. Ironically, I can go on for days about what book might suit you.

When I was called to my shop last spring because there was a break-in—broken glass, blood, overturned cases, empty drawers—I remembered, years earlier, going down to his shop one Sunday evening to the same scene.

I told him then, don't worry, we will clean it up. He was quiet, and deeply hurt. My son said the same thing to me. It was the first days of COVID—it was a bad time for blood, and it made him nervous to see how shaken I was.

It is hard to be a shopkeeper.

The New Days

I had to go into the shop early last week, well before 7:00 a.m., to catch up with the books that had just arrived and with the books that we would soon need. I have walked down to the shop from the Pike Place

Market a thousand times. For two years now, since the pandemic, it is a walk that has no company. No one says good morning, nor even signals such.

There are dog walkers and sleepy visitors and construction workers, but no one is there to say good morning. They are on the street, but it is not their street. The citizens of Seattle, the downtown cast, so to speak, have simply not yet returned to walking and working downtown.

This dark December morning, well before 7:00 a.m., I was not sure if even the somnambulant would be mobile.

But, what a surprise, a man in a full parka said good morning to me, by name. I paused and he said, I used to work in the International District but I have come back to the market, I missed the company. Then I remembered him. He was one of the best fish market countermen. I said, I am thrilled you are back.

And two blocks later, still in the morning darkness, I had to pause for a moment. They were bringing in a concrete mix for the threshold of a remodeled storefront, down by the Alexis Hotel. The foreman, a big fellow, said to me proudly, this is one of the best examples of Richardsonian architecture in Seattle.

I said, yes, I know this particular building. Where are you from, that you know about Richardson? I am from New Zealand, he said, we love history.

I walked on, past nearly three blocks of emptied storefronts—restaurants, coffee shops, clothing stores, eyewear stores—the toll of a pandemic. With any luck, the coming spring will loosen their doors, lighten their spaces, and lure someone with the best idea.

Every new shop is a new hope and a new dream. Shops will come. Some will be earnest, some too clever, some the invention of teams and some the rally of friends. They are degrees of hope, imagining they have come with just the ingredients for the time, the street, the people. Not all will make sense and not all will last—it is a difficult and silent jury.

Each is hoping for a run, a *Lion King* or perhaps *Friends*. In fishing terms, in bowling terms, each is hoping for a strike. Make no mistake—each has a dream, of bringing a shop to life.

On the Thought of Opening a Shop

What is it that you want? You want to open a shop? What do you have?

What do you know? Who would want to come to your shop? Why would they come? What would it look like?

In the very end, make it a place that you want to go. That is your best strength.

It is all a lemonade stand. Signage, counter, product, price, presentation, construction, and heart.

NO CELLPHONES
NONE AT ALL. THANK
YOU.

ACKNOWLEDGMENTS

As a shop, as a shopkeeper, and as an author, there are many people to thank.

Your own family has lived with the friendly fire of your other life, of your days too early and late, of your spirits frail or doubtful. A shop is inevitably public. And writing is insistently private. And both, in their own, intricate ways, need the truest support, in a thousand unseen ways. I am very lucky.

To work in a shop is to be a sailor. Not a pilot, as I have sometimes imagined—a pilot is separate, listening and feeling everything, but separate. To run a shop you must also listen and feel everything; it is all at your hands, in front and about you. You must be able to sail the shop in terrible weather and in dull weather, to get it out, each day, fully aloft, even if the winds are no help at all. You are the breath. And it is your part.

Many people have worked the shop. For some, it is easy or natural; for some, it is awkward; and for some, it is near impossible. It is hard to tell. And hard to do, at times. There are days when you are a one-armed banjo player, and they want tunes that you either do not know or even have. Again, I am lucky. Wonderful people have come to work, from places I did not even know, and brilliantly sailed it, day after day, out and back, caring for it as their own.

There are several people who have read the *Shopkeeping* manuscript, in many of its stages, stages when it was awkward, vain, foolish, lazy, impossible. Siblings, friends, editors, a publisher or two, best neighbors and best friends. And they have made all the difference, sending pages of notes and impressions, arguments and hopes and possibilities. They must know how crucial they are, what packets of breath and chance they ferried in, the very lines of electricity. If the book makes any sense now, if it has life and body and worth, much of that is from the care and insistence of these remarkable people.

Princeton Architectural Press was started in 1981, the same year that we opened the bookshop. We all went to the Frankfurt Book Fair, though we did not yet know each other—we were the American kids, and we had come to Europe for its brilliant design books. Eventually, we came to know everyone in design publishing and the Thursday and Friday evening gatherings grew to a legend. PA Press became its own legend, creating, representing, and publishing the very best design books in the world. It is an honor that PA Press and Jennifer Thompson, the executive editor, have agreed to publish *Shopkeeping*, I hope it knocks their socks astray!

In one personal sense, we are all shopkeepers.

A BOOK LIST

The Flower Shop: Charm,
Grace, Beauty, Tenderness
in a Commercial Context
Leonard Koren. Stone Bridge
Press, 2005
There are no ugly flowers

Interaction of Color
Josef Albers. Yale University
Press, 1963
A manual of color in space

In Praise of Shadows
Jun'ichirō Tanizaki, trans.
Thomas J. Harper and Edward
G. Seidensticker. Leete's Island
Books, 1977, first published
1933 in Japan
A parasol and a shadow

The Poetics of Space
Gaston Bachelard. Penguin,
1964, latest edition 2014
The lamp in the window

Collected Travel Writings:
The Continent: A Little Tour
in France / Italian Hours /
Other Travels
Henry James. Library of
America, 1993
The code of culture

Why a Man Should Be
Well-Dressed
Adolf Loos, trans.
Michael Edward Troy.
Metroverlag, 2011
Praise for the present,
to dress well

Geometry of Design: Studies
in Proportion and Composition
Kimberly Elam. Princeton
Architectural Press, 2001
Mathematics of proportion
and composition

The Blue Train
Lawrence Clark Powell.
Capra, 1977
Many loves of a librarian

Blue Postcards
Douglas Bruton. Fairlight
Books, 2021
The life of a postcard

Blue Trout and Black Truffles:
The Peregrinations of an Epicure
Joseph Wechsberg. Alfred
A. Knopf, 1966
The many details of
restaurant, food, and service

Giving Good Weight
John McPhee. Farrar, Straus
and Giroux, 1979
Working the Greenmarket
in NYC

White
Kenya Hara. Lars Müller,
2010
Into the very specifics
of one color

Designing Design
Kenya Hara. Lars Müller,
2007
The first perfect account
of retail design

War in Val D'Orcia
Iris Origo. D.R. Godine, 1947
The terms of keeping
oneself alive

*Terrible Honesty: Mongrel
Manhattan in the 1920s*
Ann Douglas. Farrar, Straus
and Giroux, 1995
The first American city,
the first shop

*A Piece of My Mind:
Reflections at Sixty*
Edmund Wilson. Farrar,
Straus and Giroux, 1956
Politics and words

*Sento at Sixth and Main:
Preserving Landmarks of
Japanese American Heritage*
Gail Dubrow with Donna
Graves. University of
Washington Press, 2002
Retail, in the oldest,
deepest sense

*Questions of Perception:
Phenomenology of Architecture*
Steven Holl, Juhani Pallasmaa,
and Alberto Pérez Gómez.
William Stout, 2006
Architecture, and the senses,
in space

Ideas of Order
Wallace Stevens. Alfred A.
Knopf, 1936
"A child that sings itself to
sleep / The mind"

*A River Runs Through It and
Other Stories*
Norman Maclean. University
of Chicago Press, 1976
The brilliance of language,
the brilliance of books

The Concise Townscape
Gordon Cullen. Architectural
Press London, 1961
To know the intimacy and
delight of civic order

The Odyssey
Homer, trans. Richmond
Lattimore. Harper &
Row, 1935
To each, there is an Athena,
to make the very attempt
possible

On Beauty and Being Just
Elaine Scarry. Princeton
University Press, 1999
The responsiveness to beauty
and love of truth

*Carlo Scarpa and
Castelvecchio Revisited*
Richard Murphy. Breakfast
Mission Publishing, 2017
A book that corrected the
reserve of its first iteration.
Proving, if the music is
superb, let it play. A subtle
lesson for retail.

*Signs, Streets, and Storefronts:
A History of Architecture
and Graphics along America's
Commercial Corridors*
Martin Treu. Johns Hopkins
University Press, 2012
The smile from a great bunch
of signs

A true shopkeeper

*We do what we do and we try not to do
what we do not do.*

That is a shopkeeper.